Old Monifieth
Fiona Scharlau

When Monifieth's original railway station buildings were no longer required to do service, they were relocated to a railway preservation society in Bo'ness. Only the 1905 railway footbridge remains. This section of the East Coast main line was built as part of the Arbroath- Dundee railway line in 1838. The line from Monifieth to Carnoustie is a five mile straight stretch of railway. In 1911 the station employed a staff of nine, but today it is unmanned.

With the exception of the pictures on pages 1, 11, 34, 35, 52, 53, and the back cover, all the images in this book are part of the Angus Photographic Archive.

Acknowledgements

The author would like to thank everyone who assisted her with the creation of this book, especially the team at Monifieth Library. In particular, she would like to single out the assistance of Ian Allen, former Town Clerk of Monifieth, and dedicate this book to his memory. Without his help this book would have been impossible. He donated the lantern slide collection used extensively in this publication which depicts so much of Monifieth's early history and generously gave of his time in providing the author with invaluable information. His legacy is now part of the Angus Photographic Archive and can be seen at Angus Archives, Hunter Library, Restenneth Priory, by Forfar, DD8 2SZ.

www.angus.gov.uk/history/history.htm

Further Reading

The books listed below were used by the author during her research. None of them is available from Stenlake Publishing. Those interested in finding out more are advised to contact their local bookshop or reference library.

J. Malcolm, *The parish of Monifieth in ancient and modern times*
J. A. R. Fraser, *Monifieth Golf club: the first 136 years*
Alexander Nicol Simpson, *Rambles round Monifieth*
Alan Brotchie, *Tramways of the Tay Valley*
George W Dickie, *Anecdotes of Monifieth*
Mhairi Pyott, *Monifieth Past*
Mhairi Pyott, More of Monifieth's Past
Mhairi Pyott, *Poodlie Raw, the Happy land and the Paradise*

Monifieth adopted the Burgh Police (Scotland) Act, 1892 in 1895. The village was declared a burgh by the sheriff-substitute of Forfar at a meeting on 10th February 1895 in the Gerard Hall. A provost, two bailies and a set of police commissioners were elected to run the new burgh, with a mandate to implement improvements. David Stewart was the first provost of Monifieth, holding office from 1895 to 1909. On his retirement he gifted a badge and chain of office to the next provost. In 1901 Monifieth's police commissioners became town councillors. The provost badge and chain of office are on display in the council chambers at Monifieth Library.

Introduction

The origin of the name Monifieth has been much discussed. Various meanings have been offered in the past including "the moss of the stag" and "the hill of the deer". The present day town of Monifieth lies in the southern part of ancient celtic Pictland. Carved Pictish stones were discovered in the churchyard of the parish church, later removed to the National Museum of Scotland.

The original village of Monifieth probably owes its existence to the establishment of an ecclesiastic presence by the 6th century St Regulus, or St Rule, who brought the relics of St Andrew to Angus on the way to their final resting place in the Fife town bearing his name. He erected a chapel where the bones once rested. A small settlement grew up around the chapel and subsequent church to service the needs of the ecclesiastical community. The medieval church was owned by Arboath Abbey until the Reformation. It was one of four chapels in the parish: Monifieth, Broughty Ferry, Kingennie and Eglismonichty. After the Reformation, the parish was heavily influenced by the Protestant zealot Durham of Grange, a relation of Erskine of Dun, famous for bringing John Knox to Angus.

The original medieval church was demolished in 1812 and a new, bigger church was built using recycled stones from both Balmerino Abbey and the old church. Part of the elaborate Durham of Grange family monument of 1588, previously built into the choir, was incorporated into the east gable wall.

Until the turn of the nineteenth century the village of Monifieth had changed little over the centuries. For many years Monifieth was inhabited by farmers, who rented small plots of arable land, or pendicles, from the Earl of Panmure's estate. They made their living by selling dairy produce to their large industrial neighbour, the city of Dundee. Many people kept a few cows for this purpose. The village also benefited from a reputation for the excellence of its potatoes. The links provided recreation for the locals and gentry alike, with golf being played there for centuries. In 1899 the town organized a fundraising bazaar to buy the links from the Earl of Dalhousie, raising the required money in three days. The seaside sands had hosted racing in the early 1800s. The races were attended by the finest in the county and beyond. The races took place in the spring and the summer and attracted the fashionable set who arrived in their thousands by horse, carriage and even boat. Sometimes the races concluded with a pig chase. The day ended with a dinner and a ball in Dundee. The races fell into decline and ceased in 1830. In 1839 they were briefly revived in front of 30,000 spectators, many of whom arrived by the new railway, but they had ceased finally by 1841.

Monifieth benefited from a very agreeable climate with plenty of fresh sea air, and few of the epidemics associated with the bigger towns. Many inhabitants lived to a very advanced age, so it was considered a desirable place to live.

During the nineteenth century Monifieth developed as an industrial centre. One of the most prominent industrialists was William Low who founded the company destined to become internationally renowned as James F Low & Co., Ltd as a result of Low's Foundry and the jute weaving trade. They made machines that powered the Industrial Revolution throughout Queen Victoria's Empire. During this era of industrial growth the village grew and began to change. Single storey cottages began to be replaced by tenement buildings, constructed to house the growing numbers of workers coming to the area to work in both Low's Foundry and in James C. Lyell's jute factory.

Monifieth adopted the Police Act in 1894 and became a burgh. This allowed the new magistrates to begin a programme of public health improvements such as installing pavements and street lighting. In April 1913 the city of Dundee attempted to annex Monifieth and Broughty Ferry, arguing they were merely satellites of their larger neighbour. Hearings were held at the House of Commons in April 1914. Local public opinion was against such a move but even so, former Provost David Stewart, spoke for the opposition in favour of amalgamation. Monifieth Town Council argued that the burgh had a separate identity from Dundee, and was not dependent on the city for its economic success. Defenders of separation cited the two foundries employing almost 1,000 people plus the 159 people who worked in the town's shops as evidence of their unique identity. In addition, they cited the holiday visitors, laundries, golf clubmakers, a nursery, builders, joiners, and plumbers amongst others who were based in the town. They were successful in their arguments as the Parliamentary committee decided Dundee had not proven its case. This success cost the town £24,000 to win the case.

The twentieth century saw many changes to Monifieth, not least the closure and demolition of Low's Foundry. In 1975 Monifieth Town Council became part of Dundee City Council, and has been part of Angus Council since 1996.

This view of the High Street looking west towards Maule Street pre-dates 1905 as the tramway had yet to be constructed. The roof of the Gerard Hall can be seen in the distance. The road predates the common use of tarmac in the village, and is covered in ashes.

This view of the High Street looking west shows the different character of each side of the street. The right hand side is comprised of tenements, with shops underneath, while on the left are old fashioned one storey cottages with gardens. Since 1895, the newly created Monifieth Town Council had instituted a programme of improvements throughout the town, installing kerbs on footpaths and laying down pavement on the High Street as matters of priority.

The tramway linking Monifieth to the city of Dundee was opened on 27th December 1905 by the Dundee, Broughty Ferry and District Tramways Company. The project was first mooted thirty years earlier in 1871. The new line extended the Dundee tram system from Claypots Road in Broughty Ferry to the west end of Monifieth's High Street. The decorated tram, on its first run, is stationary outside the original terminus, which was located at the foot of Union Street, near to Troup the Chemist. The tramline was extended six months later along the entire length of the High Street to a new terminus at Tay Street. The line cost £100,000 to build, and operated for only 26 years. The service closed on 15th May 1931.

Above: The tram is situated at the end of the line, where the rails and stone sets that contained them clearly just stop. After six months of operations, the tram line was extended the length of the High Street and required a new terminus in Tay Street, just outside the Royal Hotel. The trams would begin the return journey back into the city centre by simply turning the seats around to allow passengers to always face the direction of travel.

Right: The driver and conductor of the tram at the Tay Street terminus pause to pose for a photograph. The tram has turned around for the return journey to Dundee. The girl passengers on the top deck are dressed in working clothes, possibly millworkers or munitions workers.

Monifieth's shops extended the entire length of the High Street, offering a wide variety of services to the town. This grocers shop once occupied the site now belonging to Tay Court sheltered housing, at the top of Tay Street.

William Donaldson owned several properties on the High Street including his own boot shop. He was also a bailie of the town, and his shop was familiarly known as Bailie Tackets shop. Donaldson is standing in the centre of the photograph, posing with customers Tom Whyte of the Fountain Brae Nursery and John Nicoll of the burgh's cleansing staff. Note the simple display of leather boots in the shop window.

William Young ran his bakery near to Bailie Donaldson's shop. Monifieth supported a number of bakeries, and many of them commonly kept a pig in the back garden to eat the scraps. Young appears to have had a second job as the town's surveyor. His duties included checking on animal welfare.

Roads are constantly in need of repair in any era. This 1930s road repair crew was working under foreman Will Ramsay on a patch of road opposite the Episcopal Church. When Monifieth first took control of its administrative affairs under the Police Act in 1895, one of its first acts had been to macadamise the roads, and to kerb the footpaths. In 1902 the Town Council joined forces with the parish councils of Monifieth and Barry, plus the town councils of Dundee, Broughty Ferry and Carnoustie, to organise a fund-raising bazaar for improving the main road between Monifieth and Carnoustie. They hoped to straighten out many of the bends. Until the local government re-organisation in 1975, it was the responsibility of the town council to maintain the roads within the burgh.

The present day mansion at Grange is largely a Victorian building. It replaced a more ancient house which had witnessed the imprisonment, and attempted escape of the Marquis of Montrose. The Grange was once part of the lands owned by Arbroath Abbey, some of which were gifted to the Durham family by King Robert the Bruce. The Grange, as we see it today, is a product of rebuilding in 1829 and 1880. All that remains of the older house is the gateway and two ancient yew trees. The West Lodge retains a plaque of 1610 bearing the Durham family coat of arms, rescued from an inglorious period as a drain cover.

Golfing has always been a popular pastime with the ladies of Monifieth. Here we see the first ladies golf club, located at 33 Princes Street. The ladies later removed to 7 Princes Street, while no. 33 became the Licensed Victuallers Club, later the Dundee Club, who in turn moved to 12 Princes Street. The original ladies golf club house is now a private residence.

A mixed group of golfers is playing the 4th hole of the medal course around 1900. Golf has been played on the links of Monifieth since at least the 17th century, when the kirk session recorded their displeasure with two players who had dared to play on the Sabbath. Since 1869 a nine hole course has existed, played twice to make up the eighteen holes. It originally followed the path of the railway, and was a very rough course, filled with weeds and holes. There were so many rabbits inhabiting the course that a special rule was introduced to deal with them. As there was no green-keeper, members of the Artisan Club filled holes and cut the weeds in their spare time. After 1869 matters began to improve. The course was better maintained, extra holes were built on former rough ground to the north, and new clubs were established.

A group of local golfers George Wright, William McComb, William Young and their caddies are seen on the golf course. William McComb was the father of Marty McComb, golf professional at the Toledo Golf Club, who taught many top ranking American amateurs including Frank Stranahan, a millionaire.

Downie farm's old mill water wheel, powered by the Buddon Burn, was one of the many water-powered mills in the area. Many once lined the Dighty Burn, and by 1888, the growing force of industrialisation in the area had transformed the former trout and salmon steam into a filthy stinking ditch, as offensive to the eye as it is to the nostrils. Clean-up efforts have been made periodically and are continuing to this day.

During the 1930s the sands at Monifieth were popular for more than just sunbathing and paddling. The beach was also used for motorbike racing. Those involved included Provost Tyndall and James Bummy Crichton, the joint owner of a garage on the corner of Brook Street and Tay Street. Motorbike racing was not the only type of racing to take place on the links. The horse power of the motorbike had taken over from horse power in the flesh. A century earlier, the sands had provided the race course for horse races patronised by the fashionable set and landed gentry in the early years of the 19th century.

In the early 1900s Monifieth's fire brigade posed with their equipment on Hill Street, near the junction with Lorne Street. Low's foundry also had its own fire brigade, which it would lend out when needed. In the event of a major fire, such as the fire on 28th January 1934 which destroyed the Alhambra cinema, the local force was supplemented by the fire brigades of Broughty Ferry and Dundee. It took them two and a half hours to contain the blaze and the cinema, which was built of timber, was completely destroyed. Technical problems had hindered the firefighters' efforts as the pipe couplings had been incompatible. After the Alhambra fire, the town council agreed that their pipe couplings should be turned around to match those of Dundee, to make firefighting more efficient.

An early twentieth century view over Monifieth, probably taken from the parish church tower, looking west into the ancient heart of Monifieth. The entire area was once owned by Arbroath Abbey until the Reformation of the 1560s. There are a number of worn stone crosses incorporated into the garden walls of some Maule Street premises, rare survivors of ancient ecclesiastical boundary markers. The line of Hill Street can be made out behind the large house on the right. Thatched cottages are visible in the centre of the photo, while the ground around the houses on the left suggest they may be newly built.

The row of old cottages at Burnside, on the west bank of the Dighty Burn, was purchased by the town council as the site of its new high school. They were owned by the Dalhousie Estate and occupied mainly by bleachers from the nearby bleach field. The area is now largely unrecognisable due to the ongoing housing developments.

Public School, Monifieth.

Monifieth's first school after the Education Act of 1873 was built in 1878 for the Monifieth School Board. It was designed by Dundee architect David McLaren, and in its day it was considered to be one of the handsomest schools in the county. The school housed 500 pupils in eleven classrooms. It is now used as offices and is known as Invertay House. In 1928 the infant department moved to the new Seaview Primary School, after the house was purchased by the county from the Low family for this purpose.

The Bridgend of Monifieth was once a thriving community in its own right, but over the years it has gradually been swallowed up as Monifieth has expanded. The photograph shows the Milton Dairy on the east side of the Dighty Burn, and the flax mill beyond the bridge. A group of local children are gathered at the railings observing the photographer.

Apprentices are known for having their own customs, and the Monifieth Foundry apprentices were no different. These apprentices appear to be on a day out in Dundee, and posed for a souvenir in front of a photographer's studio-painted backdrop. Generations before them, another group of apprentices had mounted the daring kidnap of Mr. James Low on the day of his wedding to Miss Cox of Lochee in 1861. They had prepared and decorated an old caddie cart upon which they had secured an armchair, to which they tied Low with ropes. Four hundred employees marched him up and down the High Street in a parade headed by the works band. His release was purchased by a gift of £20 and a three day holiday. As a sign of their gratitude, the parade marched him to the station where he just caught the train to get him to his wedding on time.

William Low, a wood turner, had established the family machine-making business around 1820 when he married Jane Fairweather. Her father had owned a spinning mill at Milton and on his death her new husband and his business partner took over her fathers business, moving it into Monifieth. They also changed the focus of the business towards supplying machinery for the growing number of weaving mills, both in Scotland and India. Legend has it that William wanted to make spinning machinery to rival the best produced in England's industrial heartland at Leeds. He persuaded his artistic brother- in-law, George Fairweather, to engage in industrial espionage. William sent George to Leeds where he got a job in a foundry. During George's breaks, he secretly drew the machinery that William would later make in Monifieth. He drew the machinery patterns onto ten pieces of paper which he concealed in a specially designed hat. William and Jane presented him with a new hat every year in honour of his contribution to the new company. The drawings were on display in the Low offices for many years but have since fallen into obscurity.

By 1895 Low's Monifieth Foundry had expanded greatly and at one time employed above 500 people, making it one of the largest employers in the town. To ease the pressure on accommodation, householders were encouraged to take in as many lodgers as could conveniently be accommodated in a homely fashion. Low's Monifieth Foundry owned many properties in the town, which they rented to their employees.

These old cottages, situated on the west side of Tay Street, are now more familiar as the present site of the public library. The cottages were a quaint left-over from an earlier period of Monifieth's history, with their thatched roofs, pigsties and cow sheds. An elderly gentleman can be seen tending to his cabbages in the company of a visiting daughter and grandchild. The cottages survived until the early 1950s when the site was cleared to build the new council chambers. These purpose- built chambers were the newest in Angus.

The Royal Scots Greys were one of the regiments that recruited in Angus. They were a distinguished cavalry regiment, named after their usage of only grey horses. Since 1971 they have been part of the Royal Scots Dragoon Guards. They are seen here riding through Monifieth in 1895 on their way to their base at the army training camp at Barry Buddon, between Monifieth and Carnoustie. Barry Buddon is a large area of woodland and heath which has been used a military training camp since the 1860s.

The produce of the farms, vegetable gardens and dairies in Monifieth parish had a ready market in Dundee. Early potatoes and vegetables were supplied along with milk, many of them transported in little donkey carts such as this one from nearby Ardownie Farm.

The Panmure Lodge of the Ancient Order of Shepherds is marching west along the high street in 1900. They are passing outside the South Church Halls, opposite the tenements of Foundry Terrace, accompanied by local children. The Order was a friendly society, established in 1888, with Samuel Low as their treasurer. Friendly societies provided a mechanism for ordinary people to save or make provisions for infirmity, old age, death or burial, and were mutual benefit societies owned by their members.

The bays along the north coast of the River Tay estuary can be treacherous, and have witnessed the grounding, or wrecking, of many vessels. One such was the Crown of Jersey, which ran aground in the early 20th century, carrying a cargo of apples, which quickly disappeared! A hundred years earlier the bay was the location of less innocent pastimes, as it was a favourite landing spot for smugglers. Many kegs of whisky and brandy are said to have been hastily buried in the sand and never recovered.

Right: The South Church on Hill Street was built in 1872 to provide new accommodation for the Free Church and the United Free Church. Additions have been made over the years, including the round tower and a gallery in 1884, and transepts in 1904. The first minister at the South Church was Reverend Robert Macgregor.

Below: Monifieth constructed a striking war memorial to the 59 men of the burgh and parish who died in the First World War. It was built on the site of a roadside thatched cottage once well-known for its troutie well. The gable end in the background belonged to Jamie Baird's inn. The money for the memorial was raised by public subscription and it was unveiled in June 1922 by the Lord Lieutenant of the County of Forfarshire, the Earl of Strathmore. The bronze figure representing peace was created by sculptor Herman Cawthra, and the plinth was designed by Charles G. Soutar. The grounds were landscaped by Bailie Dick's company.

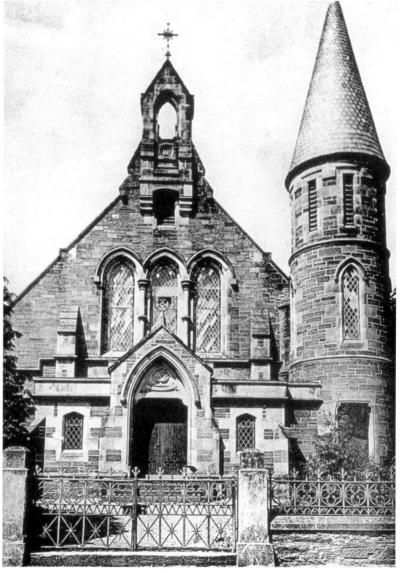

The Reverend James Gerard Young endowed Monifieth with two gifts, the Gerard Hall and the Gerard Cottage Hospital. He was born in Edinburgh in 1821, the son of a legal man. Monifieth was his second and last charge. Young came to the town in 1855, where he worked tirelessly in many areas for the benefit of the local community. Amongst his many roles he was the first chairman of the Monifieth School Board, clerk to the Dundee Presbytery and a staunch advocate of the sunday school movement. It was in this cause that he gave the money gifted to him for his semi-jubilee to start the building of the Gerard Hall. He also left the bulk of his estate to found a cottage hospital in the burgh. He died on 4th October 1899, and the Gerard Cottage Hospital opened in October 1902. The hospital was in use until 1969. It is now a residential home for the elderly.

Convalescent soldiers are seen here enjoying a game of bowls. Monifieth operated a thirty bed Red Cross hospital throughout the First World War. It was said to be finely equipped and splendidly managed. At the start of the war many large houses, including Glamis Castle, offered their services as convalescent hospitals for wounded soldiers.

Scotland's east coast seaside towns were popular holiday resorts in the early years of the twentieth century. A group of Edwardian women and children are enjoying a paddle in the water by the sunlit sands of Monifieth. The town's links and beaches were a popular destination for Dundonians looking for fresh air after the smoke of the city. The good train and tram service to Monifieth made the town easily accessible to many.

Children can't resist the simple pleasures of the sand and the sea. Sea bathing, boating, fishing and golf were especially popular with holidaymakers and daytrippers alike.

The Panmure Hotel was built specifically to cater to Victorian and Edwardian holidaymakers who flocked to Monifieth in large numbers to enjoy the beach and the golf course.

Monifieth Golf Club, Monifieth

In 1858 the Monifieth Golf Club was founded for the village artisans. Membership was very popular amongst the foundry workers. They assisted in maintaining the golf course prior to the employment of a green-keeper in 1869, their expenses being met by the Panmure club.

36

205925 J.V.

Starter's Box and Club Houses, Monifieth Golf Course

The present golf course starters box was built in 1911. The original first tee was moved to this location when the railway line cut off part of the old course in 1838. The first tee was originally situated on the site of a garden in Dalhousie Gardens. The golf clubs on Princes Street can be seen in the background.

Monifieth House on Hill Street is an imposing early Victorian house built by Doctor James Carmichael Lyell, an antiquarian and businessman. In 1878 he established the jute spinning mill on the links beside the railway line, becoming known as the Little Foundry, or the Albert Works. In 1901 Monifieth House was bought by Provost David Stewart, who renamed it Chellwood. It is now a hotel, and much of its garden ground has been developed for housing.

It is a mark of respect, common to most Scottish burghs, to place a lamp outside the home of the current provost. This one was located outside Monifieth House, or Chellwood, during the term of office of Provost David Stewart. Another pair of lamps was bought by the town council during the Second World War from the burned-out Majestic Cinema in Dundee. They were originally located outside the Queens Hotel in the Nethergate, Dundee. Until recently, two lamps were located on Hill Street. One stood outside the former home of Provost Cameron Watt, while another was located further along Hill Street outside the home of Ian Mortimer, the last provost of Monifieth. Provost Watt's lamp has now been relocated to Monifieth Library.

Tay Street, Monifieth.

77318.J.V.

A view of Tay Street looking towards the High Street around 1914. In the background are some of the Edwardian villas built in the town's boom period at the beginning of the twentieth century. Much of the construction of villas and houses was carried out by building companies owned by Bailie James Tullis and by J. B. Hay. The removal of Bailie Tullis firm from Monifieth caused a slump in the building trade.

Monifieth High Street in the early 1920s. The only wheeled vehicle on the street is a cart in the distance. In the middle right of the picture is a Gothic style tenement, built up from a single storey cottage in 1911. It was owned by Miss M. Christie, a confectioner, and designed by Bruce, Proudfoot and MacRae of Cupar.

A timeless view of children enjoying playing in the East End Park in the 1950s. The park was built on the links, adjacent to the site of the Low & Duffs Little Foundry. A caravan park now occupies the site. In 1904 the town purchased land at the west end of the links from Mr. Anderson of the Grange as a pleasure ground. It is still in use as a playground for a new generation of Monifieth children and visitors.

Balmossie Mill photographed in 1908. It was one of the many mills on the Dighty Burn, its mill lade serving the bleach fields at Milton of Monifieth. The mill is believed to have been built using old carved stones from the medieval chapel of Eglismonichty in its construction. The lade was filled in around 1947.

A High Street scene showing Foundry Terrace to the left. The terrace was built by the Low family to house workers from the Monifieth Foundry. On the opposite side of the High Street is a row of impressive tenements known as Peebles Buildings. It was owned by two brothers of that name who ran a grocers' business in the town. Another row of foundry workers tenements could be found fronting Reform Street. They had the quaint, but obscure, nickname of Poodlie Raw.

At the corner of High Street and Tay Street lies the memorial garden adjacent to the library, once the site of a row of thatched cottages. The boys are sitting on the wall of the former police station. The site was later the TSB Bank and is now a local authority office.

High Street at its junction with Union Street looking east, with John Wallace's cycle shop in the foreground. It was demolished around 1930. The cycle shop was adjacent to the Dundee Eastern Co-operative Society Ltd. In 1923 the lease of the Co-op was taken over by the town council who used the building as their offices. The building had moveable wall partitions, allowing great flexibility in its use.

HIGH STREET, MONIFIETH   D 726

Looking towards the former council chambers, now the library. Beyond the council chambers can be seen the old house and shop which once stood on the corner of Tay Street. It was demolished in 1973 and sheltered housing built in its place. Beside the council chambers is the new Alhambra Cinema, built to replace the earlier Alhambra which was a wooden construction on Tay Street. This part of the High Street was demolished, and now houses a former petrol station, awaiting redevelopment.

HIGH STREET, MONIFIETH

B. 1485

A view of High Street taken from near the junction with Tay Street. Hendersons was originally two shops, one of which was Geekies the butcher who slaughtered their own animals at the back of the property. The council chambers have yet to be built at the time of this photograph as the site is still occupied by the row of single storey cottages, with the cinema visible beyond. The large tenement beyond the cinema was known as Taylor's Buildings. This building, and its turreted neighbour, has since been demolished.

In 1878 Doctor James Carmichael Lyell and Charles Lyell built a flax mill on the links, on the south side of the railway, as well as two rows of cottages for their workers, the Victoria and Albert Terraces, better known as the Bricklands or the Brickies. In 1902 Low & Duff purchased the site and moved their Albert Works from Dundee to Monifieth. The workforce was much smaller than its larger neighbour, hence the nickname of the Little Foundry. In addition to foundry work, Low & Duff were also brass finishers. Samuel Low had interests in both Low & Duff and J F Low & Co.s Monifieth Foundry. Here we see a group of Little Foundry workers outside the factory office. The men are probably the works quoiting team, and it is likely that the quoits they played with were a product of the foundry.

A group of workers and apprentices from Low & Duff seated outside, with Maule Street in the background. The square tower of St Rules can just be seen over the rooftops. Many of these workers would have lived in the factory cottages known as the Bricklands. When Low & Duff took them over from Lyell's flax mill, they had deteriorated into slum conditions. They were described as a dark blot with a bad reputation, where the residents were living in squalor and filth. Low & Duff gutted the cottages, completely renovating them into attractive homes once more. They have since been demolished.

A group of unidentified Monifieth Foundry workers in a large workshop, many of the men smoking cigarettes or pipes. In 1911 the Foundry was entirely rebuilt and equipped with the most up-to-date tools. It prided itself on running a modern and efficient business. When the demand for spinning equipment declined, the foundry diversified into other products such as baking equipment. The company closed in 1980.

A mixed group of foundry workers, possibly taken during the First World War. The younger men had gone to fight as soldiers, and the women of the Monifieth area were recruited into the foundry, which had switched its production to bombs and mines.

Ashludie, Monifieth.

Ashludie House lies at the core of the modern day Ashludie Hospital. It was originally one of the area's principal estates. The last family to live on the estate was that of wealthy Arbroath flax spinner Alexander Gordon, who had moved to Arbroath in 1847 from Montrose, and commenced operations as a flax spinner at the Burnside Mill. Active in the public life of Arbroath as a town councillor, chairman of the school board and the library management committee, he retired from business in 1897 and devoted his time to improving the Ashludie Estate before dying on 26th June 1911. The house, originally built around 1866, was designed by James McLaren in the style of a large Jacobean style mansion, set in 124 acres of grounds.

As the twentieth century progressed, the hospital continued to expand, building wards in the garden ground surrounding the main house. This view shows patients enjoying fresh air on the specially designed verandas, believed to be vital in the treatment of tuberculosis.

The flax spinning mill on the Dighty at Milton was built in 1788, and extended in the early nineteenth century. It is the oldest surviving water-powered flax mill in Angus. It was owned in the early nineteenth century by Baxter and Fairweather but was largely disused by the 1850s. Robert Kerr of the Grange converted it to a flour mill in 1872, and leased it to Robert Reid & Son. By 1888 its function had changed again, and it became a scutching mill for Carmichael and Dalgleish. One of its last functions was as a heckling mill in the early years of the twentieth century.

The flax mill at Milton was the last mill on the Dighty Burn before it flowed into the sea. In the nineteenth and early twentieth century the Dighty was badly polluted by the various industries using it. The mill building has subsequently been used as the tram depot and as a carpet factory. After a fire in 2006, the building may enjoy a new lease of life as housing.

A crowd assembles for the 1950 Christmas Carol service in front of the Christmas tree outside the former municipal offices, at the top of Tay Street. Local church choirs led the singing from hymns projected onto a screen. The crowd kept warm with braziers placed at suitable intervals.